Teaching Notes

Contents

What Is It?

The Animal Party

The Best Sandcastle

Don't Jump on the Bed, Fred!

Can You Get Our Ball?

Tortoise! Tortoise!

Introduction

The *Snapdragons* series is a rich mix of different kinds of stories presented as picture books with expertly written text carefully levelled to provide reading practice at each stage in Key Stage 1.

This set of six books at Stage 2 will help to develop the early reading skills that children need to become competent readers. The six simple stories are told in patterned language with a predictable structure. The stories introduce children to early key words as well as useful vocabulary relating to the different contexts. Children are encouraged to develop early reading skills in mapping spoken word to written word.

Three of the stories at Stage 2 are based in familiar settings: the home, the garden and the beach. They reflect everyday life and the readers will quickly identify with the family members and recognise their experiences. The other three stories in this set transport the readers into the world of fantasy, involving animal characters and even aliens from another world.

The simple plots at Stage 2 allow children to learn how stories develop and each one contains an element of surprise. Children are encouraged to look at the illustrations for visual cues to the words in the text, and to find out what is happening in the story. The picture book presentation will also encourage children to tell the story in their own words and develop their oral skills.

How to introduce the books

Before reading the story for guided or independent reading, always read the title and talk about the picture on the cover.

Go through the book together, looking at the pictures and talking about them. If there are context words (listed in the chart on page 4) that are new or unfamiliar, point them out and read them with the children. Read the story to the children, encouraging confident children to join in with you.

This booklet provides prompts and suggestions for using the books in groups and for guided, group and independent activities, matched to text, sentence and word level objectives. There are also separate Guided Reading Cards available for six titles at each stage. Suggestions are also provided for speaking and listening activities, writing activities, and cross-curricular links. You can use these suggestions to follow on from your reading or at another time.

Reading notes are also provided in each book. They can be found on the inside front and back covers of each book. These suggest friendly prompts and activities for parents or carers reading with their children at home.

Reading skills

Stage 2 develops:
- an understanding of text and the way it behaves
- book-handling skills
- the ability to link text to pictures
- an understanding of narrative sequence
- phonological awareness, i.e. the awareness that letters are symbols for sounds
- early writing skills.

Vocabulary chart

Stage 2		
What Is It?	Year R High Frequency Words	a and big it no said
	Context words	lampshade Bip Bop hat dress small seat wide tunnel alien
The Animal Party	Year R High Frequency Words	a all can come I like my the to yes you
	Context words	party bark dog quack duck hoot owl moo cow baa sheep animal
The Best Sandcastle	Year R High Frequency Words	and is it my no on the to we went
	Context words	sandcastle beach more bigger sand flag shells stones seaweed mine
Don't Jump on the Bed, Fred!	Year R High Frequency Words	all and can come dad I in like look mum on said the yes you
	Context words	jump Fred sofa chairs house stairs around down best bed stop garden
Can You Get Our Ball?	Year R High Frequency Words	a all can dad mum get he in it he the to up was we went you
	Context words	ball tree football looked up again roof ladder
Tortoise! Tortoise!	Year R High Frequency Words	a can come I in is it no of said was
	Context words	tortoise asleep shell woke today squirrel windy autumn robin cold winter frog wet spring sunny summer

Curriculum coverage chart

Stage 2	Speaking and listening	Reading	Writing
What Is It?			
NLS/NC	4a, 4b	T8, S3, W4	T11
Scotland	working towards Level A	working towards Level A	working towards Level A
N. Ireland	Activities: c, g Outcomes: a, d	Activities: e Outcomes: e, f	Outcomes: b, g
Wales	Range: 5 Skills: 6	Range: 2, 5, 6 Skills: 1, 2	Range: 2, 3 Skills: 3, 8
The Animal Party			
NLS/NC	T7, 4a, 4b	T8, S1, W9	T11
Scotland	working towards Level A	working towards Level A	working towards Level A
N. Ireland	Activities: c, Outcomes: d	Activities: e Outcomes: c, f	Outcomes: b, c
Wales	Range: 5 Skills: 2	Range: 2, 5, 6 Skills: 1, 2	Range: 2, 7 Skills: 3, 8
The Best Sandcastle			
NLS/NC	3a, 3c, 3e	T7, S1, W11	T12
Scotland	working towards Level A	working towards Level A	working towards Level A
N. Ireland	Activities: f, g Outcomes: a, c, d, e	Activities: b, c, e Outcomes: d, e	Outcomes: a, b
Wales	Range: 1, 3 Skills: 2, 3, 4, 5, 6	Range: 2, 5, 6 Skills: 1, 2	Range: 2, 3 Skills: 1, 2, 3, 8
Don't Jump on the Bed, Fred!			
NLS/NC	3a, 3e	T8, S3, W10, W14	T14
Scotland	working towards Level A	working towards Level A	working towards Level A
N. Ireland	Activities: f, g Outcomes: a, c, d, e	Activities: b Outcomes: b, c, d, f	Outcomes: a, b, c
Wales	Range: 1, 3 Skills: 2, 3, 4	Range: 1, 2, 5, 6 Skills: 1, 2	Range: 2, 3, 7 Skills: 1, 3, 8
Can You Get Our Ball?			
NLS/NC	1c, 1d, 1e	T4, T9, S1, W6	T14
Scotland	working towards Level A	working towards Level A	working towards Level A
N. Ireland	Activities: f, g Outcomes: a, c, d, e	Activities: b, c Outcomes: b, c, d, e	Outcomes: a, b, c
Wales	Range: 1, 3 Skills: 2, 3, 4	Range: 4, 5, 6 Skills: 1, 2	Range: 2 Skills: 1, 2, 3, 8
Tortoise! Tortoise!			
NLS/NC	1d, 1e	T3, W3, W9	T11
Scotland	working towards Level A	working towards Level A	working towards Level A
N. Ireland	Activities: a, f, g Outcomes: a, b, c, d, e	Activities: b Outcomes: b, c, d, e	Outcomes: a, b, c
Wales	Range: 1, 3 Skills: 2, 3, 4	Range: 1, 2, 5, 6 Skills: 1, 2	Range: 7 Skills: 2, 8

What Is It?

Reading the story

Introducing the story

- Look at the front cover and read the title. Ask the children: *What sort of creatures are these?*
- Look at the title page and ask: *What is this?* (a lampshade)
- Look through the illustrations and ask: *Where are Bip and Bop? What do they think the thing is?*
- Ask the children to say what they think the thing is. (a lampshade)

During reading

- Praise the children who read the repeated phrases confidently, "Is it a…", "No, it is too…".
- Prompt the children to use the pictures and initial sounds to work out the interest words.
- Encourage the children to read the speech bubbles on pages 14 and 16 in an expressive tone.
- On page 16, ask: *Do you know what an "alien" is?*

Observing Check that the children:
- notice the change from the question, "Is it…?" to the statement, "It's…" on page 8
- track the text, carefully pointing at each word
- use the illustrations and different sized fonts to help them read the interest words.

Group and independent reading activities

Text level work

Range sci-fi/predictable structure/patterned language

Objective To locate and read significant parts of the text, e.g. bold, enlarged words (T8).

- Ask the children to look through the book page by page and point to the words: "big", "small", and "wide".
- Ask: *How is this word different from the others?*

Observing Do the children understand how the way the word is printed reflects its meaning?

Sentence level work

Objective That words are ordered left to right and need to be read that way to make sense (S3).

You will need the following word cards:
Is, it, a, hat, dress, seat, tunnel
No, it, is, too, big, wide, small

- Ask the children to work with a partner. One child sequences the first group of words; the other child sequences the second group of words to answer the question.
- Encourage the children to re-read the sentences carefully, checking they make sense.

Observing Do the children take turns to sequence their words? Do they check their sentences make sense?

Word level work

Objective To link sound and spelling patterns by using knowledge of rhyme to identify families of rhyming CVC words (W4).

You will need pens and whiteboards.

- Write the words "bip" and "bop" on the board. Demonstrate how to change the initial sound to create two new words, e.g. hip and hop.
- Ask the children to experiment with changing the initial letter on their whiteboards to make pairs of new words.

Observing Can the children hear the difference in the vowel sounds?

Speaking and listening activities

Objectives Use language and actions to explore and convey situations, characters and emotions (4a); create and sustain roles individually and when working with others (4b).

- Discuss what sort of story this is, e.g. ask: *Is this a "real life" story? Do you think it really happened?*
- Discuss what Bip and Bop thought the lampshade was.
- Ask the children to suggest other things the lampshade could be.
- Ask the children to work in pairs and act out what Bip and Bop say and do, using the story and any new things they have thought of.

◄► **Cross-curricular link**
Numeracy: mathematical development, using size language such as "big" and "little"

Writing

Objective To understand that writing remains constant, i.e. will always "say" the same thing (T11).

You will need pens and whiteboards.

- Write a sentence from the story on the board, e.g. *No, it is too big.*
- Discuss how the sentence is written in the story (e.g. how the last word is bigger). Discuss that the way it is written does not affect what it says.
- Change the final word to one not used in the story, and encourage the children to come and write it in different ways on the board.
- Ask the children to suggest other words that could be written in similar ways to reflect their meaning, e.g. thin, high, low, fat.
- Ask the children to write the sentence on their boards and experiment with writing the final word in different ways to reflect its meaning.

The Animal Party

Reading the story

Introducing the story

- Look at the front cover and read the title. Ask the children: *What do you think the story is about? What sort of party will it be?*
- Look through the illustrations and talk through the book. Ask: *What animals are the children dressed as? Can you point to the word that says dog/duck/owl, etc?*
- As you look through the illustrations, read the animal noises in the speech bubbles with the children. Encourage them to join in with you.
- Return to the title page and read the title together.
- Read pages 2 and 3 together. Ask: *Who says the words in the speech bubble? Who says the words, "Good! Come to my party."?*

During reading

- From page 5 onwards, praise the children who respond to the change of words, e.g. from "Good! Come to my party" to "Good! Come to the party." etc.
- Prompt the children to use the pictures to work out the animal names.
- Encourage the children to read the speech bubbles in an expressive tone.

Observing Check that the children:
- track the text in the right order, pointing carefully to each word
- read the high frequency words with increasing confidence
- notice what is happening in the illustrations.

Group and independent reading activities

Text level work

Range fantasy/predictable structure/patterned language

To locate and read significant parts of the text, e.g. speech bubbles (T8).

- Ask individual children in the group the questions in the story, e.g. "Can you hoot like an owl?" Ask the child to find the correct speech bubble and read it.
- Ask: *How can you tell who is saying this in the story?*

Observing Do the children trace the speech bubble to the correct character?

Sentence level work

Objective To expect written text to make sense and to check for sense if it does not (S1).

You will need the following unfinished sentence strips and additional word cards:

Can you bark like a...?	dog
Can you quack like a...?	duck
Can you hoot like an...?	owl
Can you moo like a ...?	cow
Can you baa like a...?	sheep

- Give the children 3 or 4 of the sentence strips, and all the word cards. Ask them to read the sentences and complete them with the correct word card.
- Prompt the children to re-read the sentences carefully, checking they make sense.

Observing Do they re-read the sentences to check they make sense?

Word level work

Objective To recognise the critical features of words, e.g. shape, length (W9).

You will need words cards:
dog, duck, owl, cow, sheep

- Ask the children to group the words according to their length. Ask: *Which is the longest word? Which words are the same lengths?*

Do the children recognise the length of the words by their shape, or need to count the letters?

Speaking and listening activities

Objectives To use knowledge of familiar texts to re-enact or re-tell to others, recounting the main points in correct sequence (T7); use language and actions to explore and convey situations, characters and emotions (4a); create and sustain roles individually and when working with others (4b).

You will need masks or puppets for a: dog, duck, owl, cow, sheep

- Give the children the puppets or animal masks.
- Choose one child to invite the animals, and re-enact the story in sequence. Prompt the children to make the animal sounds and imitate their movements.

◀▶ **Cross-curricular link**
Creative development: exploring colour, texture and shape by making animal masks; use in role-play

Writing

Objective Through shared writing, to apply knowledge of letter/sound correspondences in helping the teacher to scribe, and re-reading what the class has written (T11).

You will need pens and whiteboards.

- Ask the children to suggest other animals they would like to invite to the Animal Party, and the noises they would make.
- Write the sentence on the board: "Can you...like a...?"
- Choose one of the animals from their suggestions and model how to fill in the gaps in the sentence. Ask the children to write these words on their whiteboards.
- Some children may be encouraged to write the complete sentence.

The Best Sandcastle

Reading the story

Introducing the story

- Look at the front cover and read the title. Ask the children: *What do you think the story is about? Do you think the picture shows the best sandcastle?*
- Look through the illustrations and talk through the book.
- On page 2, ask: *Where are the children?* On pages 4 and 5, ask: *What are they doing?*
- Ask: *What does the girl do to her sandcastle? What does the boy do to his sandcastle?*
- On pages 14 and 15, ask: *What is the sea doing? What do you think might happen to the castles?*
- Return to the title page and read the title together. Ask the children to read the story.

During reading

- Praise children who read the enlarged, bolder words in an expressive tone.
- Remind them to use the pictures to support their reading of interest words.
- Encourage the children to read the speech bubbles in an expressive tone. Ask the children how they would say the words in the speech bubbles if they were making the best sandcastle.

Observing Check that the children:
  - track the text in the right order, pointing carefully to each word
  - use their knowledge of phonemes to help them work out words
  - check the illustrations to help them read the interest words.

Group and independent reading activities

Text level work

Range familiar setting/predictable structure/patterned language

Objective   To use knowledge of familiar texts to re-enact or re-tell to others, recounting the main points in correct sequence (T7).

● Ask the children to work with a partner. Ask each to take the part of the brother or the sister and then act out the sandcastle competition.

Observing   Do the children recall the sequence of events in their re-enactments?

Sentence level work

Objective   To expect written text to make sense and to check for sense if it does not (S1).

You will need word cards to make the following sentences:
We went to the beach.
We made sandcastles.

● Give the children the muddled-up word cards. Ask them to put them into order to make two sentences from the story.
● Prompt the children to re-read the sentences carefully, checking they make sense.

Observing   Do they re-read the sentences to check they make sense? Do they need to refer to the book to make their sentences?

Word level work

Objective   To make collections of personal interest or significant words and words linked to particular topics (W11).

● Look together through the book and discuss the things that are usually only found on a beach, e.g. seaweed, shells, sandcastles.
● Ask the children to find each of the words in the story.

Observing   Do the children use their knowledge of initial sounds to identify the words?

Speaking and listening activities

Objectives Take turns in speaking (3a); take different views into account (3c); give reasons for opinions and actions (3e).

You will need an object relating to the story for the children to hold while they take their turn to speak, e.g. a shell.

- Ask the children to sit in a circle. Pass the shell around the group and ask the children to say what they liked or disliked about the story.
- Ask the children if they have been in any competitions with their brothers, sisters, or friends.

◀▶ **Cross-curricular link**
Creative development: exploring shape, form and space in two or three dimensions

Writing

Objective To write labels or captions for pictures and drawings (T12).

- Ask the children to imagine they are having a sandcastle competition. Tell them to draw their own sandcastle, and to add labels to the drawing to describe what they put on the castle.
- Some children could use the book to find some of the words they need, e.g. "sand", "flag", "shells", "stones", "seaweed".
- Some children may be able to write a sentence about their sandcastle.

Don't Jump on the Bed, Fred!

Reading the story

Introducing the story

- Look at the front cover and read the title. Ask the children: *What do you think the story is about?*
- Turn to page 2, and read "Boing" to the children.
- Look through the illustrations and talk through the book. Ask: *What does Fred do all the time? How can we tell he jumps about all day long?* (He is wearing different clothes.)
- Ask the children who they think is speaking in the speech bubbles.
- Ask: *What do you notice about how the lines of words are written?*
- Return to the title page and read the title together. Ask the children to read the story.

During reading

- Praise the children when they follow the text carefully with their fingers.
- Encourage the children to read the speech bubbles in an expressive tone.
- Ask the children to point out "Boing' when they see it again (on page 8).

Observing   Check that the children:

- understand the different ways speech is written in the story, by asking them to point out speech bubbles on the page
- use their knowledge of phonemes to help them work out words
- check the illustrations to help them read the interest words.

Group and independent reading activities

Text level work

Range   familiar setting/predictable structure/patterned language

Objective   To locate and read significant parts of the text, e.g. speech bubbles, enlarged words (T8).

● Ask the children to look through the book again, and to read aloud the words in speech bubbles.
● Ask: *How do you know who is saying the words in the speech bubbles?*

Observing   Do the children understand that the speech bubble points to the character that says the words?

Sentence level work

Objective   To know that words are ordered left to right and need to be read that way to make sense (S3).

You will need word cards to make the following sentence:
He jumped down the stairs

● Give the children the muddled-up word cards. Ask them to put them into order to make sense.
● Ask the children to find the sentence in the story, and compare their own sentence with the way it is written in the book.
● Ask them to say why the words in the story are not always in straight lines.

Observing   Do the children understand that the text effects still need to be read top to bottom and left to right in order to make sense?

Word level work

Objectives   To learn new words from their reading and shared experiences (W10); To write letters using the correct sequence of movements (W14).

You will need pens and whiteboards.

● Ask: *Where does Fred jump in the house?*
● Draw up a list on the board: sofa, chairs, stairs, bed.
● Ask the children to find each of the words in the story.
● Ask them to practise writing them on their whiteboards.

Observing Do the children use their knowledge of initial sounds to differentiate between "chairs" and "stairs"? Do they form the letters using the correct sequence of movements?

Speaking and listening activities

Objectives Take turns in speaking (3a); give reasons for opinions and actions (3e).

● Ask the children about what they are allowed to do at home, e.g. Ask: *Do you jump on the furniture? Do you do anything at home that you are told to stop doing?*
● Encourage the children to give reasons why Fred was told not to jump around the house.

◀▶ **Cross-curricular link**
Physical development: moving with control and coordination

Writing

Objective To use experience of stories as a basis for independent writing, e.g. re-telling, substitution, and through shared composition with adults (T14).

● Write the sentence "I like jumping" on the board.
● Discuss other activities the children like doing, e.g. running, playing, throwing, dancing. Write a list on the board for reference.
● Ask the children to write the sentence, substituting "jumping" with other words from the list.

Can You Get Our Ball?

Reading the story

Introducing the story

- Look at the front cover and read the title. Ask the children: *What has happened to the ball?*
- Ask the children to look through the book, focusing on the illustrations.
- Ask: *What do you notice about the words in this story? How should you hold this book while reading it?*
- Return to the title page and read the title together. Ask the children to read the story.

During reading

- Praise the children when they follow the text carefully with their fingers.
- On pages 8 and 9, ask: *Why can't Mum get the ball this time?*
- On pages 14 and 15, ask: *Why can't Dad get the ball?*
- On page 16, ask why the children say: "Oh no!" Ask: *What is different about the text on this page?*

Observing Check that the children:
- understand the different ways speech is written in the story, by asking them to point out speech bubbles on the last page
- can give reasons for events in the story.

Group and independent reading activities

Text level work

Range familiar setting/predictable structure/patterned language

Objectives To notice the difference between spoken and written forms through re-telling known stories; to compare 'told' versions with what the book 'says' (T4); To be aware of story structures, e.g. actions/reactions, consequences, and the ways that stories are built up and concluded (T9).

- Ask the children to work with a partner and take turns to re-tell the story by looking at the illustrations.
- Encourage them to add reasons as they re-tell the story, e.g. "The ball went in the tree because the wind blew it."
- Ask: *What is different about how you describe the story?*

Observing Do the children understand that the illustrations add detail that is not in the text?

Sentence level work

Objective To expect written text to make sense and to check for sense if it does not (S1).

You will need the following sentence strips with a word missing, and word cards:

We went to...football.   play   went
The ball went...in a tree.   up   on
Mum went to...our ball.   get   can
The ball...on the roof.   was   all

- Give the children the sentences and two word cards. Ask them to read the sentence and add a word to make sense.
- Ask the children to find and read the sentence in the story.

Observing Do the children read their sentences to check for sense before finding it in the text?

Word level work

Objective To read on sight high frequency words from YR (W6).

You will need pens and whiteboards.

- Write the following words from the text onto the board: "our", "get", "went", "said".
- Ask the children to start from page 2 and find each of the words in the story. Ask them to count the number of times each word occurs, and write them on their whiteboards.
- Wipe the words from the board and the whiteboards, and ask the children to write the words again without looking in the book.

Observing Do the children remember how to spell the words correctly? Do they form the letters using the correct sequence of movements?

Speaking and listening activities

Objectives Organise what they say (1c); focus on the main point (1d); include relevant detail (1e).

- Ask the children to say why the ball kept getting out of reach.
- Ask the children what they can play when it is windy, and what games the wind would spoil.

◄► **Cross-curricular link**
Knowledge and understanding of the world: How can we tell it is windy? What can we see, feel or hear?

Writing

Objective To use experience of stories as a basis for independent writing, e.g. re-telling, substitution and through shared composition with adults (T14).

- Talk about where the ball went in the story.
- Ask the children to suggest other places a ball could be blown on a windy day.
- Write some of the children's suggestions on the board, e.g. "The ball went on the road." "The ball went into the pond/river."
- Ask the children to write a sentence describing where the ball went, and to illustrate it as a very windy day.

Can You Get Our Ball?

Tortoise! Tortoise!
Reading the story

Introducing the story

- Look at the front cover and read the title. Ask the children what they think the story will be about.
- Look together through the book, focusing on the illustrations. Point out the "Zzzz! Zzzz!" on page 3. Ask the children what they think this means.
- Ask: *What do you notice about the weather in the pictures?*
- On page 6, ask the children to point to the words "windy" and "autumn". Continue through the story, asking the children to point to the words that describe the weather and the season.
- Return to the title page and read the title together. Ask the children to read the story.

During reading

- Encourage the children to read the questions and answers in an expressive tone.
- As the children read, ask them to explain why Tortoise can't come out of his shell.
- On pages 12 and 13, ask: *What is different about how the words are written on these pages?* (They are in speech bubbles.)

Observing Check that the children:
- understand the different ways speech is written in the story, by asking them to point out speech bubbles on the last pages
- use the illustrations to help them read the names of the seasons
- track the text confidently while reading.

Group and independent reading activities

Text level work

Range   fantasy/familiar setting/predictable structure/patterned language

Objective   To re-read a text to provide context cues to help read unfamiliar words (T3).

- Write "spring", "summer", "autumn" and "winter" on the board.
- Ask the children to look through the book and find the words in the text.
- Ask the children to identify how they find the words. (Do they use the illustrations or match the word in the text with the word on the board?)

Observing   Do the children use more than one cue to find the correct word?

Sentence level work

Objective   To know that words are written left to right and need to be read that way to make sense (W3).

You will need the word cards to arrange into this sentence:
Come out of your shell

- Give the children the muddled-up word cards. Ask then to arrange the words into a sentence that makes sense.
- Ask the children to find and read the sentence in the story.

Observing   Do the children read their sentences to check for sense before finding it in the text?

Word level work

Objective   To recognise the critical features of words, e.g. shape, length, and common spelling patterns (W9).

You will need pens and whiteboards. The outline shapes of the words below on card or paper:
autumn, winter, spring, summer

- Write the following words from the text on a board: "autumn", "winter", "spring", "summer".
- Ask the children to find each of the words in the story.
- Ask the children to write the words on whiteboards, and to draw carefully around each word so that their shapes are shown.
- Show the children one of the prepared outline shapes and ask them to pick which it is on their whiteboards. Repeat with the other shapes.

Observing Do the children recognise the shapes of the words on sight?

Speaking and listening activities

Objectives Focus on the main point(s) (1d); include relevant detail (1e).

- Ask the children to say why it was not a good idea for Tortoise to come out of his shell in the autumn, winter or spring.
- Discuss keeping animals as pets with the children. Ask them to say how they look after the needs of their own pets.

◀▶ **Cross-curricular link**
Knowledge and understanding of the world: similarities, differences, pattern and change (what the seasons are like)

Writing

Objective Through shared writing, to apply knowledge of letter/sound correspondences in helping the teacher to scribe, and re-reading what the class has written (T11).

- Discuss the illustrations in the story that show how the weather changed from season to season.
- Ask the children to help you write a sentence about each season.
- Write, "In autumn it is…" on the board and encourage the children to finish the sentence.
- Repeat with the remaining seasons.

Oxford Reading Tree resources at this level

There is a range of material available at a similar level to these stories which can be used for consolidation or extension.

Stage 2

Teacher support
- Teacher's Handbook
- Big Talkabout Cards
- Big Books for each story at Stage 2
- Guided Reading Cards for Stage 2 Stories
- Take-Home Cards for each story
- Extended Stories
- Storytapes / More Storytapes
- Stories Video
- Context Cards
- Workbooks 2a and 2b
- Sequencing Cards Photocopy Masters
- Group Activity Sheets Book 1 Stage 1–3
- ORT Games Stages 1–3

Further reading
- Oxford Reading Tree Storybooks for Core Reading
- Fact Finders Unit A
- Branch Library: Wildsmith Books Stage 2 Packs A & B
- Glow-worms Poetry

Electronic
- Clip Art
- Stage 2 Talking Stories
- ORT Online www.OxfordReadingTree.com
- Floppy and Friends

For introducing phonics
- First Phonics Stage 2

For developing phonics
- Alphabet frieze, Tabletop Alphabet Mats, Alphabet Photocopy Masters
- First Story Rhymes
- Card Games

OXFORD
UNIVERSITY PRESS

Great Clarendon Street, Oxford OX2 6DP

Oxford University Press is a department of the University of Oxford. It furthers the University's objective of excellence in research, scholarship, and education by publishing worldwide in

Oxford   New York

Auckland   Cape Town   Dar es Salaam   Hong Kong   Karachi
Kuala Lumpur   Madrid   Melbourne   Mexico City   Nairobi
New Delhi   Shanghai   Taipei   Toronto

With offices in

Argentina   Austria   Brazil   Chile   Czech Republic   France
Greece   Guatemala   Hungary   Italy   Japan   Poland   Portugal
Singapore   South Korea   Switzerland   Thailand   Turkey
Ukraine   Vietnam

Oxford is a registered trade mark of Oxford University Press in the UK and in certain other countries

© Oxford University Press 2004

The moral rights of the author have been asserted

Database right Oxford University Press (maker)

First published 2004

British Library Cataloguing in Publication Data

Data available

Cover illustrations by David Mostyn

Teacher's Notes: ISBN 978 0 19 845516 5

10 9

Page make-up by Fakenham Photosetting, Fakenham, Norfolk

Printed in China by Imago